SUMMARY
Of
American Dirt

A Novel by
Jeanine Cummins

Summary Created
By

Cosmic Publications

©2020 Cosmic Publications

Note to readers

This is an unofficial summary & analysis of Jeanine Cummins "*American Dirt"* designed to enrich your reading experience.

Buy the original book on Amazon.com

The information in this book has been provided for educational and entertainment purposes only.

The information contained in this book has been compiled from sources deemed reliable and it is accurate to the best of the Author's knowledge; however, the Author cannot guarantee its accuracy and validity and cannot be held liable for any errors or omissions. Upon using the information contained in this book, you agree to hold harmless the author from and against any damages, costs, and expenses, including any legal fees, potentially resulting from the application of any of the information provided by this guide. The disclaimer applies to any

OUR FREE GIFT TO YOU

We understand that you didn't have to buy our summary, but because you did, we are very happy to give you something absolutely free.

Scan the QR Code to get free Access.

TABLE OF CONTENTS

Book Summary Overview

Lydia Quixano Perez is a Mexican woman living in Acapulco with her journalist husband Sebastian and their eight-year-old son, Luca. Lydia owns a small bookshop, which gives her opportunities to surround herself with the books she loves while also allowing her to escape the mundane reality through reading. Following a violent cartel attack, sixteen members of Lydia's family get murdered, including her husband. The massacre takes place in the family's backyard where their generation have gathered to celebrate the birthday of a 15-year old girl, Luca's cousin. The only ones to survive are Lydia and Luca. Behind the gruesome attack on her family is none other than Javier Crespo Fuentes, head of the dominant cartel and a frequent client of Lydia's bookstore. Since Sebastian's newspaper article came out identifying La Lechuza (The Owl), as head of the dominant cartel in Acapulco, Lydia knows her family is in danger. Her only option is to get out of Mexico. What complicates matters more is the fact that

Javier, La Lechuza has been a close friend of Lydia and a frequent client of her bookstore. As Javier's influence and reach extend all over the country, the mother and son will need to transform into migrants and ride La Bestia, the "death train," which crosses Mexico towards the northern border with the United States. Joining the other Central American migrants on their route to the border, Lydia and Luca will develop a unique friendship with two sisters from Honduras, Soledad, and Rebecca, who will become their road companions and lifelong friends. Finding money in her dead's mother bank account will help Lydia cover all the road expenses for her and Luca, including the fee they had to pay to the Coyote, who will lead them across the desert to their new lives in the United States. The many dangers they will have to face on their journey while being hunted by a ruthless criminal and estranged from their home and the entire family will permanently scar Lydia's and Luca's souls and break their whole existence forever.

Setting for the Story

Mexico is the primary setting for this novel. We begin in Acapulco, where the main book protagonists were living before the cartel attack and across the country towards the northern border with the United States. Passing through Chilpancingo, Huehuetoca, Guadalajara, Nevolato, Mexico City, and finally Nogales, the novel depicts the realities that migrants face on their turbulent journeys towards their new life destinations. From jumping on the deadly train La Bestia, surviving cartel attacks and facing arrest by local police, to risking their lives in the dangerous heat of the desert, their struggle to stay alive will leave its mark on their lives forever. The epilogue depicts the main protagonists in the United States, where they are trying to adjust to their new life circumstances.

Story Plot Analysis

The novel starts in nowadays Acapulco Mexico, where Lydia's entire family gets murdered in an armed attack by the dominant cartel. The only one to survive is her son Luca. Most of the narrative is in the third person and depicts Lydia's journey to escape from Mexico together with her son. The plot of the novel follows the exposition in which the author introduces us to the main characters, which are Lydia and Luca, and to the setting, which is Mexico. As the rising action occurs, we get to follow Lydia and Luca throughout their entire survival journey from Mexico to the United States, in a breathtaking ride of La Bestia throughout the major cities which connect Acapulco to Novalato. The story has many pivotal moments, and among them, one stands out as having the most substantial impact on the reader. The moment that the migrants get caught by the local cartel in Sinaloa creates the fear in all those following the story that some of the main protagonists might end their journey abruptly and violently. Following the death of Beto, the action cools down and heads towards its final moments. The resolution will find Lydia, Luca, and the two sisters in Arizona, where they all live with the girls' uncle while trying to put back together with the scattered pieces of their broken lives.

The main idea which the writer wishes to transmit her readers throughout the pages of her book is that when speaking about migrants we should always remember that: *"these people are people" and if given a better life alternative, " these people would never leave their homes, their cultures, their families, even their language, to venture into tremendous peril, risking their very lives, all for the chance to get to the dream of some faraway country that doesn't even want them."*

Main and Secondary Character List

Lydia Quixano Pérez – The female protagonist of the novel and the mother of Luca. Up to the cartel attack, she leads a comfortable life in Acapulco where she owns a bookstore.

Luca Quixano Pérez – Lydia's son and her only family member that survived the cartel massacre which killed her entire family.

Sebastian Quixano Pérez– Lydia's husband and former reporter. He dies in the cartel attack

Javier Crespo Fuentes – The head of the dominant cartel in Acapulco and the one responsible for the killing of Lydia's family.

Rebeca and Soledad –Two sisters from Honduras who Lydia and Luca meet in their journey. They will become lifetime friends and they will live together even once arriving in the U.S.

Lorenzo- A former cartel member that Lydia and Luca meet at the Family Home in Huehuetoca and who will follow them throughout their entire journey.

Beto – A 10-year-old boy that Lydia and Luca meet while trying to embark on La Bestia. He will join them in crossing the border but he will not survive the desert and die from asthma.

El Chacal (Juan Pedro) – the coyote that will help the group of migrants cross the desert to the United States

Carlos – Sebastian's friend from Chilpancingo who will help Lydia and Luca hide till finding a way to send them to Mexico City

Meredith – Carlos 'American wife

Rey- The minister at the Emigrant House in Huehuetoca

Angela – The assistant at the hospital where the father of the two sisters is in a coma

Ricardo Montanero-Alcan – the doctor from Navolato who helps Lydia, Luca, Rebecca and Soledad to get safe to Navolato and after to Hermosillo.

Marisol - a Mexican woman that got deported from the United States where she was living with her two daughters. She is part of El Chacal's group of migrants

Nicolas – A Mexican student who got also deported from the U.S. where he was studying at the university. He will cross the border together with El Chacal and the others.

Slim –. One of the five men which El Chacal brings to the apartment on the last evening before the desert crossing

Choncho – Slim's brother

Ricardin - Slim's son who will get injured in the desert and left behind with his uncle Choncho

Paola – the cashier at the bank in Nogales who helps Lydia take out her mother's money.

Ricardo Montanero-Alcan – the doctor from Navolato who helps Lydia, Luca, Rebecca and Soledad to get safe to Navolato and after to Hermosillo.

Marisol - a Mexican woman that got deported from the United States where she was living with her two daughters. She is part of El Chacal's group of migrants

Nicolas – A Mexican student who got also deported from the U.S. where he was studying at the university. He will cross the border together with El Chacal and the others.

Slim –. One of the five men which El Chacal brings to the apartment on the last evening before the desert crossing

Choncho – Slim's brother

Ricardin - Slim's son who will get injured in the desert and left behind with his uncle Choncho

Paola – the cashier at the bank in Nogales who helps Lydia take out her mother's money.

Chapter by Chapter Analysis

Chapter 1 The Killing of The 16

Three men are responsible for the killing of 16 people in an armed attack in Acapulco. The only ones escaping are an eight-year-old boy, Luca, and his mother, Lydia, who were hiding in the shower at the time of the assault. The attack takes place in the backyard of Lydia's mother, where the whole family gathered to celebrate the birthday of Yenifer, Luca's cousin. Shaken and terrified by witnessing the brutal killings of all her beloved ones, Lydia calls the police.

Chapter 2 The Police Arrive

The police arrive at the scene of the attack, and upon interrogating Lydia, they conclude that the shooters came after Sebastian Perez Delgado, Lydia's husband. Sebastian was a well-known reporter in Acapulco whose articles have mostly centered on the local cartels. Lydia knows that the only one who could have orchestrated a bloodbath of this magnitude was Javier Crespo Fuentes, head of the dominant cartel, *Los Jardineros*. More than that, Lydia also knows that the police will do nothing to protect her, as most of the officers were on the mafia's payroll and receiving regular money from the local cartels. Realizing that the survival of her son is only in her hands, Lydia starts moving fast. Entering the house to search for a piece of luggage in which to pack some things for the road, she will find 15,000 pesos under her mother's bed mattress, which she packs together with some clothes, bathroom toiletries, and her mother's favorite brown bag. After first considering driving Sebastian's car, Lydia realizes that his orange Beetle would turn them into an easy target and decides that she and Luca need to find another way of disappearing from Acapulco.

Chapter 3 Unwanted Attention

Grabbing from the car Sebastian's backpack and his New York Yankee hat together with some of Luca's shoes and old t-shirts, Lydia and her son head towards the local bus station. Lydia's appearance as a moderately attractive but not beautiful woman traveling with an unremarkable-looking boy is what helps them blend in with the other bus riders and not draw too much attention on themselves. Stopping at the bank, Lydia takes out all the money she had left in the deposit, buys some clothes for Luca and a small machete for protection, and decides to take a hotel room under a false name. Choosing the Duquesa Imperial hotel for the night, the mother and son will feel safe for the moment. What Lydia doesn't know is that as soon as they will pick up their key and head towards their room, the front desk clerk will inform someone about their presence in the hotel.

Chapter 4 Back in Time

When looking in the past, the narrative depicts how Javier Crespo Fuentes and Lydia first met when he came to the book shop that she owned. Lydia has owned the store for ten years, and she had stocked it not only with popular books that would sell but also with some of her best-loved secret treasure gems. Whenever a book would marvel her, she would add those secret ranks of unique books. There were only a few buyers that would ever choose among Lydia's books, and Javier was one of them. The fact that he chose two of her favorite books opened the dialogue between them. They soon realized that except for liking the same books, they had many other things in common, including a strange and fictional condition: they both couldn't prevent themselves from jumping off high things. Their friendship deepened in time as Javier kept returning to the shop. He began to confide in Lydia with stories about his personal life, including his wife, daughter, and even his mistress. The two develop a mature friendship that passes the initial flirtatious stages.

One evening, while talking with Sebastian about Acapulco's recent changes caused by the cartels' violence and control of the city, Lydia realizes that the leader of the new dominant cartel is none other than her friend, Javier.

Chapter 5 Present Time

Chapter five brings us back to the present time, in Lydia and Luca's hotel room. Waking up in the middle of the night, Luca is terrified by finding himself in an unfamiliar place. As it's already almost five in the morning, Lydia decides that they should not sleep anymore and hit the road. Before continuing their journey, Lydia orders breakfast for her and Luca, but the delivery boy hands her a mysterious package. Lydia freezes in panic at the thought that no one was supposed to know where they are, and still someone managed to find out. As she will soon discover, inside the package, there's an English-language copy of Love in The Time of Cholera, a book she once discussed with Javier and one of their favorites. Together with the book, there is also a letter where he confesses the killing of her family. Realizing that Javier knew where they were, it put them in great danger. Lydia and Luca get dressed quickly and leave the hotel by the service stairs.

They plan to head to Denver, Colorado, where an estranged uncle of Lydia has been living for a long time.

Are you enjoying the book so far?

If so, please help me reach more readers by taking 30 seconds to write just a few words on Amazon

Scan me

Or, you can choose to leave one later...

Chapter 6 The Bus Station

Lydia attempts to convince one of the hotel shuttle drivers to take her and her boy to the bus depot, but the driver rejects her request until she offers him some money for the ride. They hope that by going to the bus station in Diamante district, they might be able to lose their trace, and they assume that everybody will be looking for them at the central terminal downtown. Arriving at the bus station, Lydia buys two one way tickets for her and Luca. The direction is Mexico City and then Denver. While waiting for the bus to arrive, Luca demonstrates his geography knowledge and tells Lydia all the information that he knows about Denver. As Lydia starts to remember, Luca was born with an intrinsic sense of position on the globe and a capability to lodge forever in his brain anything that he might see on the globe. Sometimes Lydia would bring Luca to the bookstore just so that he could amaze the tourists with his incredible knowledge and information regarding any place in the world.

Chapter 7 Leaving Acapulco

As mother and son board the bus, they are both happy to be able to leave Acapulco safe. While Luca is sleeping, Lydia remembers her trips to Mexico City with Sebastian and the way he was speeding in his orange Beetle around the gentle mountain curves, on the beautiful curves of the road that she and Luca are now on. Without Waking Luca, Lydia spreads the map. She analyzes the way ahead of them, knowing that the path to Mexico City will have at least one roadblock occupied by Los Jardineros. Arriving in Chilpancingo, they disembark from the bus, and Lydia thinks of how to find Carlos, one of Sebastian's college roommates who was living in the city with his wife. In the meantime, she and Luca head to an internet café where Lydia tries to figure out the safest alternatives for them to reach Mexico City without being intercepted by the cartel. While looking for Sebastian's friend on Facebook, she finds a Pentecostal church that he is usually attending on Sundays and decides to head there. Entering the church, she waits for the mass to start and sees Carlos with his wife, Meredith. The two take Lydia and Luca to their home, and while preparing tea for them, they start thinking of a safe way to help the woman and child get to Mexico City unscathed. As a group of fourteen Indiana Missionaries is visiting the city for spring break, Carlos thinks to hide Lydia and her son in the shuttle taking the American girls to Mexico City. Meredith first opposes the plan considering that she would be placing the young girls in too much danger, but she finally gives in to the idea understanding that Lydia and Luca will end up getting killed if she won't help them.

Chapter 8 La Lechuza

The narrative returns in time to the evening that Lydia realized that Javier and La Lechuza were the same people. Tormented on how to confess to her husband that Javier is her friend from the bookstore, Lydia waited for the next morning to tell Sebastian everything. Following her confession, he took the day off from work to discuss with her the situation more in-depth. Shocked and shaken, Lydia finds herself torn between the need to accept that the man she thought she knew so well was a cold-blooded criminal. At the same time, Sebastian realizes that there are strong feelings behind his wife's and Javier's friendship and that they share a strong bond caused by both losing their fathers.

While still trying to accept Javier's new image, Lydia confronts him with the first occasion when he visited her at the shop. Presuming that she had known the truth about him long before, Javier confesses his love for her and tries to explain his status in the cartel and why he is in no position to change his life and leave the cartel.

Chapter 9 Stay Hidden

While waiting for the missionaries' bus to leave for Mexico City, Lydia and Luca need to stay hidden in Carlos and Meredith's house and not raise any suspicion on themselves. The days roll by with Luca reading on the couch while Lydia spends her time at an old IBM computer where she checks for headlines coming out from Acapulco. Reading through the stories of local violence and killings, she also notices that there are many articles regarding the increased roadblocks across the area. Traveling within cities is relatively safe, but the real danger comes from going outside of them. Lydia thinks of plane flights as an alternative to the roadblocks, and as a last resort, she also studies the freight trains the Central American migrants ride across the length of the country. From Chiapas to Chihuana, the terrifying train La Bestia is the traveling method that only the poorest and most destitute of people attempt to use due to its many dangers and inhuman traveling conditions.

On the following Wednesday, Carlos takes the day off from work to drive one of the church vans in which Lydia and Luca will ride too. During the ride, one of the American girls offers to make Lydia's hair the same as theirs, caught in two French braids. In the meantime, Luca takes a nap on the floor beneath the seats. On the way, the bus stopped at a roadblock by two young men who are part of Javier's cartel. It all ends well as the men are not able to see Luca, who was sleeping on the floor. When they ask about Lydia, they tell her that she is one of the local counselors brought to take care of a sick girl.

Chapter 10 The Tram

As Lydiaarives in Mexico City, she parts ways with Carlos and Meredith, but not before thanking them for saving her and her son's lives. Lydia understands how problematic the whole situation must have been for Meredith and the considerable risk the woman took to save them. The mother and son will next embark on the tram, which is supposed to deliver them at the domestic flight terminal. As Luca has never been on a tram before, he is fascinated by the whole new. Getting in front of the woman at the ticket counter, Lydia tells her that they decided to go on a spontaneous trip. Anywhere from Nuevo Loredo, to Ciudad Juarez or Tijuana. Deciding to buy two tickets for Tijuana, Lydia faces a new and unexpected problem: she cannot board on the flight with Luca as she doesn't have with her the boy's birth certificate. Confused and desperate, Lydia exits the airport with her son and takes a moment to think about what their next move should be. She chooses to head towards the National Library Miguel Lerdo de Tejada,

36

a building of extreme beauty that Lydia used to love coming to when she was studying literature in college. Sitting in front of one of the computers in the library gives Lydia the idea that by disgusting themselves as migrants, she and Luca could stand a chance to reach the border without being caught by the cartel. Researching more about La Bestia, the train they need to ride with the other migrants crossing Mexico, Lydia is terrified by the many ways the train can kill its illegal passengers. Willing to trust that among the half-million people that survive La Bestia each year there will also be them, Lydia decides that her plan is sound. She and Luca set out to search the commuter train to Lecheria, the city where the migrants usually gather before boarding on La Bestia.

Chapter 11 La Bestia

Before taking the train, Lydia checks her mother's credit card in the hopes that she might find some more money to use on the road. As the number pops up on the screen, Lydia is shocked to see that there was much more money than she had even dared to hope for: $10.000. Lydia remembers with affection how her mother has been a calculated woman who loved to work and make her own money, who had always emphasized the importance of being independent and saving money.

Taking the commuter train to Lecheria, the mother and son arrive in the city and search the location where the Migrant House was supposed to be. They find the place closed and find out that the site moved to a nearby town, Huehuetoca. Because it's late already, Lydia decides they should spend the night in a cheap motel. The next morning they woke up very early and set out north towards Huehuetoca. As Luca starts asking questions about La Bestia and why they don't buy tickets to embark on it, Lydia explains to him that La Bestia is not a train for people. It's a commercial train that migrants ride illegally by jumping on it while the train keeps moving. Walking along the train rails, the mother and son encounter a group of migrants and start talking to a man named Nando from Honduras who was traveling with his brother. He tells Lydia how they plan to jump on the train and what method he found to work better. As the train rounds the distant bend and comes into view, Lydia and Luca witness the shocking way that the two men jump on the train. Lydia realizes that she and Luca will have to do the same, and the thought terrifies her.

Chapter 12 The Migrant House

Arriving in Huehuetoca, they quickly find the Migrant House, where they are warmly welcomed by a minister called Rey, his help Nestor and Sister Cecilia. After they get a bit of rest and eat lunch, Lydia and Luca go to Sister Cecilia's office, who is responsible for registering them. Holding some paperwork and a file folder in front of her, the woman starts asking Lydia questions about the situation, which brought them there. As Lydia tells the nun the whole truth, the woman tries to offer a little comfort and a prayer for their protection on the arduous journey ahead, while also warning Lydia about being careful of what she talks and to who.

At night, Luca wakes up, and while trying to reach the bathroom, he hears father Ray and Nestor talking angrily to a young man in the men's bunk room. As the young man heads down the corridor, Luca notices a tattoo with three blood-red droplets on the man's ankle. As Luca returns to the bedroom, his mother asks what the shouts were about. Luca is worried but cannot say anything.

Chapter 13 Heads

Lydia's memory wonders back in time, a time when Acapulco was still a safe city to live. The first time a dead boy's head appeared in town, it was a big deal for everyone till the next head turned up. By the time their number reached a dozen, everyone was already used to heads being found. Sebastian's article *Acapulco Falls* was the trigger that announced the beginning of the cartel terror that will soon take over the city. To Lydia, the change felt sudden, as like going to bed and waking up in a completely unknown city. As her husband's article felt a bit too melodramatic, he explained to her that words couldn't express enough the atrocities that were going on in their city.

Being in the Migrant House in Huehuetoca, with her son sleeping in her arms, Lydia wonders if those first heads that appeared had anything to do with Javier.

Waking up the next morning, Lydia finds Luca already awake near her, and she feels the smell of cooked food. In the breakfast room, as Lydia and Luca eat their breakfast, they hear the discussion between two women who are talking about the incident that had happened the night before. An immigrant man, the one Luca saw when he woke up to use the toilet, had raped a young girl from the house, and the priest, with his help, threw him out. The women continue by saying that from what they know, the man was a member of a cartel that alerts Lydia and makes her worry.

Chapter 14 Rebeca and Soledad

Leaving Huehuetoca and heading north once again, following the trail of La Bestia, Lydia thinks of a safe way for her and Luca to board the train. A couple of hours north of the migrant shelter, Lydia and Luca encounter two teenage sisters. Both of them are very beautiful, but the older one is dangerously so. Starting a conversation, the sisters introduce themselves as Rebeca and Soledad, who was the older one. They are from Honduras and are trying to get to their cousin Cesar who lives in the United States. They continue by telling Lydia and Luca the tricks they found to help them jump safely on La Bestia. The key to their method is a location they saw where the train slows down for a curve allowing them to jump on it from an overpass nearby. The sisters ask the mother and child to join them, and Lydia agrees to feel that she can trust them. As the train pulls itself into view, the four of them get ready, and following the girl's advice, they all end up safe on top of La Bestia.

Chapter 15 Lives in Danger

One year before Sebastian's murder, Mexico was already one of the most dangerous countries in the world for journalists. Following the discovery behind Javier's true identity, both Sebastian and Lydia tried to take a minimum of precautions. Sebastian decided never to have a daily routine while Lydia became hypervigilant to any sign of danger. Before Sebastian publishing his article in which he portrays Javier as the head of the dominant cartel, Lydia and Sebastian discussed whether the article would put their lives in danger or not. Considering that her husband depicted Javier in a fair and flattering way, Lydia calmed her fears regarding the reaction that her "friend" might have upon seeing himself in the newspaper.

Turning back to riding on top of La Bestia, Lydia and Luca witness as the train ambles from west to north, and the landscape rolls beneath them shifting colors. Periodically the train stops, making the migrants alert to any sign of police control. When the train stops at San Miguel de

Allende, Lydia and Luca follow Soledad and Rebeca into the town in search of something to eat. The city center is colorful, festive, and full of people eating *tortas* and drinking coke, and to Luca, it seems one of the strangest places he has ever seen. The sisters use their charms to find dinner quickly, and the four of them enjoy a hot ball of spaghetti Bolognese. As the night covers the city, the four travelers find a bunch of municipal benches where they stretch themselves, trying to get some rest.

Chapter 16 The Pacific Route

Early in the morning, the four travelers join the other migrants waiting for the train, while Lydia feels exhausted from lack of sleep. The plan is to follow the Pacific Route because, as the sisters explain Lydia, everyone warned them that all the other ways are dangerous because of cartels. The southbound train doesn't stop in San Miguel de Allende but is travels slowly, so everybody manages to board on it with ease. On top of the train, Luca and Rebeca start to talk about the lives that both of them had left behind. They also spoke of the events which led the sisters into leaving their homes and trying to reach the United States. Their father was working in a hotel in San Pedro Sula a city that offered more work opportunities than the village where the sisters were living with their mother and grandmother. Rather than trying to find protection from the cartels, the girls decided they should move to their father's place in the city. Their lives didn't get easier there as Soledad found herself harassed by a man called Ivan, who proclaimed himself her boyfriend.

Worried about his violence and threatens, Soledad decided that to protect her sister, they should leave the city. Leaving behind a letter to her father in which she explains her decision, Soledad sends a text to her cousin Cesar in Maryland asking for help. He offers his support and pays a coyote $8,000 to cross the sisters over the border to the United States.

Chapter 17 Lorenzo

Lydia and the sisters arrive in Celaya at another Migrant House, where they spend a few days and where Soledad realizes she's pregnant with Ivan's child. The priest leading the house tries to give a word of encouragement to the twelve migrants in the house, and his speech does the job of energizing the migrants and steeling their resolve. Luca, Lydia, and the girls leave the house and search for an overpass from where they can jump back on La Bestia.

While on the train, Luca notices a boy with a familiar face who is staring at his mother. In no time, Luca recognizes who the boy is even before seeing the tattoo with blood drops showing from under his socks. Seeing that the man is taking out his phone just to throw one more glance towards his mother, makes Luca warn Lydia about the fact that he had recognized someone on the train. He continues by telling her about the man he saw getting kicked out from the Migrant House in Huehuetoca, and the tattoo with the tree blood drops he had noticed on his ankle. Starting to panic, Lydia thanks Luca for telling her about the man and quickly assesses the situation. It doesn't take long for her to realize that the boy is a cartel member and that he has most probably already recognized them. Soon after, the boy approaches Lydia and Luca and introduces himself as Lorenzo. He continues by telling Lydia that he knows who she is and how everybody is looking for them at Javier's request. Lydia manages to get a breath of air as Lorenzo tells her that he's not planning to turn them in. He is on his way to Los Angeles, where he wants to start a new life, far from his past deeds and the cartel.

Chapter 18 Danilo

Arriving in Guadalajara, Lydia and the two sisters decide to stay together with a group of four other migrants they had met on the train. The men seem kind and safe, with their steep accents of Central Americans. The women prefer their company over the many dangers that are lurking from behind each corner. Lorenzo follows the group as well causing more worry to Lydia When the group reaches El Verde, a mustached man named Danilo approaches the group and lets them know that he wants to walk with them and protect them from the dangers that might appear on the way. The men cheer his offer, but Rebecca and Soledad exchange worried glances as they know better than trusting foreign men that offer their help without wanting nothing in return. Danilo tries to calm their fears and tells them that his only intention is to protect them and offer them a pleasant memory to think of when remembering Guadalajara. He confesses that as a teenager, he stole and destroyed a truck for which he never got caught and punished, and that is why his wish is to give back to others in the act of penance. While on the road, trying to find out more information from Lorenzo, Lydia hears that soon after Sebastian's article appeared in the newspaper, Javier's daughter committed suicide as she had been unaware of her father's business.

Chapter 19 Martha's Death and The Sisters Father

Lydia is shocked after hearing what happened to Javier's daughter and understanding now better the motif behind Javier's revenge against her family. She knows how vital Marta was to her father, and he remembers all the beautiful ways in which Javier was describing her. Lydia reanalyzes all the details from the night before Sebastian's article got published and realized that they couldn't predict that something so unpredictable would happen. Lydia feels sorry and guilty for Martha's death, but this will not let her forgive Javier for killing sixteen of her family members.

As the group of migrants continues their walk through the city, Danilo proves himself to be of real help for them and reacts against all the threats which appear, making Lydia feel as though Danilo has saved their lives at least seven times on the road.

Later that day, upon arriving at a local shelter, the two sisters take advantage of finding a phone and call their father. Unable to reach him, they find out from the receptionist at his working place that he got brutally stabbed one week before as he was coming into work and was now lying unconscious in the national hospital.

Finding the number from the hospital, Soledad calls there and asks to receive some information about her father's situation. One of the nurses is willing to help them and tells them that their father suffered considerable damage to the brain and was now in a coma. The nurse warns the girls not to come to the hospital as they could risk their lives and promises to look after their father.

Chapter 20 Worry and the Continued Journey

Later that night, Lydia is in for another bad surprise, as Lorenzo arrives at the shelter where her, Luca, and the sisters were staying. Before going to sleep that night, Lydia thinks of the connection that bonded her to the two sisters. Who now feels like family to her. Although they haven't discussed the idea of traveling together till reaching their destination, it was an arrangement that all of them intuitively understood. Lydia is even imagining how her future would look if she and Luca would restart their American lives in the Arizona desert with the sisters instead of going to Denver. Also awake, the sisters can't sleep worrying about the last part of their road. A woman from the shelter warned them of how dangerous the state of Sinaloa is for women, is famous for its expertise at disappearing girls and the vigor of the local cartel. Soledad is determined to get safe with her sister in the States so that she can honor their family's sacrifice and suffering.

As soon as the sun rises, the two sisters, together with Lydia and Luca, get back on the train. Lydia feels a lot of relief at the thought of leaving the city and Lorenzo behind. As La Bestia crosses into Sinaloa, Soledad feels more and more nausea from her pregnancy but also from all the stress she's been experiencing and throws up over the edge of the train. Upon reaching a tiny village, the train approaches a camp of migrants. Trying to jump on the train, one of them gets sucked beneath the wheels of the beast as the other migrants gather around the trails to assess the body pieces of the severed man. Although Lydia tries to stop Luca from watching the gruesome scene, he has already seen how the man got cut in half.

Leaving the death scene behind, Lydia and Rebeca discuss about the way they will cross the desert and since Lydia hasn't found yet a coyote for her and Luca, the sisters suggest that they could all go together with the one that their cousin Cesar found. His name is El Chacal, and he is waiting for the girls to call him when they arrive in Nogales. He is supposed to be the best the girls say, and Lydia is convinced. All of a sudden, as the train approaches Culiacan, the monotony is broken by loud voices that announce the police. All the migrants start grabbing their things and jumping off the train. In a few moments, Lydia realizes that the agents that she sees are not there to enforce law and order and knows that she cannot count on her and Luca being Mexican citizens. Feeling that they are in great danger, she grabs Luca, and both of them start to run for their lives.

Chapter 21 Police Raid

The migrants' attempt to escape is useless, as the "police" have surrounded the train. There is nowhere for the migrants to go or hide as there is no town or bush around where they can find protection. While running with Luca, Lydia falls and breaks her ankle and forced to stop as the sharp pain is too intense for her to continue running. Luca returns by her side, afraid that his mother got shot but felt relief as he sees that there is no trace of blood on her body. As he looks after Rebeca and Soledad, he sees the girls still running in the distance. One by one, all the migrants get caught, handcuffed, and embarked into two trucks. One of the migrants is outraged of the situation and asks to speak with the man in charge. As an officer approached, the man tells him that he is a Mexican national, and should not be detained. The officer says to the man that there is no one in charge. That all the agents are in charge and are allowed to hold whoever they wish.

Lydia and Luca are allowed to stay together, but the two sisters are taken in another car despite Lydia's attempt to declare them her daughters so that they could all be together.

Chapter 22 Paying for Freedom

The ride is dark and frightening for all of them, and Lydia is trying not to overthink about what Soledad and Rebeca could be enduring. As the trucks stop and the doors open, Lydia soon understands that they are not at a detention center, but an anonymous warehouse. There is no doubt left now that it was not the police who caught them. Soon after, Rebeca and Soledad are brought there also with the other car. The girls do not look well, and both have visible signs of being beaten and raped. Rebeca is bleeding from her forehead and her mouth is swollen. Both their bodies are limp, and they don't have any reaction as a guard moves them in line with the other migrants. One of the officers asks the migrants to tell if any of them are Mexican citizens. One of the migrants that is caught lying about his origins is quickly shot in the head. When Lydia's turn arrives to tell about her background, she gives enough information to prove that she is indeed a Mexican national. The commander invites her and her son into his office. The commander then takes the money from her wallet in exchange for their freedom. Luca doesn't want to leave Soledad and Rebeca behind and since the girls don't have any money, Lydia decides to pay for them too. The money covering their freedom is almost all the money that Lydia had left for the journey.

Chapter 23 The Doctor Ricardo Montanero-Alcan

All the money that Lydia is left now after paying for the sisters too is $243. The amount is too little for the road ahead, but as the doors to the warehouse open, Lydia doesn't think about the money. All she thinks about now is getting away from there as fast as possible. All of them keep running, without a clear direction, but just with the bright idea that they must get away before the men change their minds and come after them. As the night falls, a car approaches them, and a doctor named Ricardo Montanero-Alcan offers them a ride to Navolato and medical help at his clinic. Afraid to trust the man in the beginning, the women accept the water and cookies that he offers them, and in the end, they decide to trust him and ride with him to Navolato. They safely arrive at a hotel where they will spend the night, but that same night Soledad loses her baby. The next day the doctor drives them to Culiacan, from where they embark La Bestia again.

Chapter 24 - 300 Miles Away from Nogales

Arriving in Sonora, the desert starts to assert itself, and Luca can feel the smell of the ocean. Everything around them feels dusty and dry, and Luca feels thirsty all the time. It is the first time throughout their ride that his mother doesn't have to convince him to drink water. With his geography knowledge, Luca informs his mother and the girls that they are very close to the northern border, just 300 miles from Nogales. Entering the city of Hermosillo, the four need to jump again from the train as the other migrants alert them about another police ride. Running among the narrow streets and past shaded gardens, they find a local woman who helps them hide in her barn and covers their traces as the police knock at her door looking for them. After the police pass the house, Lydia decides that it is safer for them to stay in the barn at night and leave early the next morning. Exhausted and desperate, Rebeca starts to cry and tells her sister that she just wants to get back home and leave everything behind her. Soledad warns her that there is no home left for them, and they just need to keep ongoing. They all continue to stay in the shed while the woman that helped them hide is having dinner inside the house with her son. At night she gives them some food and asks them to leave the barn before daylight.

Chapter 25 Beto

Before the dawn sets, Lydia, her son, and the sisters enter Hermosillo and walk till they arrive at a large park with a fountain in the middle. As Luca takes a moment to refresh in the cooling water, Lydia splurges on a cup of coffee. After spending the night in the park, early in the morning, as soon as the shops open, Lydia buys two pairs of hiking shoes for her and Luca, to help them in crossing the desert.

Walking along the railway tracks, they see many migrant campsites, and some of them appear to be permanent. It will take a few days till the next train will arrive, and Lydia uses the time there to observe the reality around her. The wait there together with the other migrants feels like the most extended wait Lydia has ever experienced. After Luca told her how close they are to the border, she can already feel the desert air and the taste of freedom.

As the train approaches the station, the engineer slows down as like to allow all the migrants to board, and everybody manages to get safely on. When the second line of track approaches, a boy riding the train coming from the opposite direction jumps down and hops on the train that Lydia and Luca were riding. As the boy approaches them and starts talking with Luca, Lydia notices that the boy who was around Luca's age didn't have any luggage with him, and his face was unburned from the sun. She starts being circumspect as she doesn't understand what to make of him. She wonders why he is alone at such a young age and why he is so friendly with Luca. The boy has problems with his breath and manages to calm an asthma attack by using an inhaler he had in his pocket. The boy further introduces himself as Beto. He is ten, and he is traveling by himself. Soledad also takes an interest in the little boy and starts asking him questions, curious to find out more about his background. They find out that Beto was born near a garbage dump in Colonia Fausto Gonzales, and his mother was a garbage picker. He had another brother who died squashed by a track when he was eleven, and Beto is afraid now that turning this age will be a bad omen for him too.

Two hours later, while a plane flies low preparing to land, the train enters Nogales.

Chapter 26 Feeling Safe in Nogales

Being in Nogales makes everyone feel safe as though they had already arrived in the United States. Soledad starts crying with relief at the thought that they managed to come so far, and are still alive. Beto invites them all for lunch, offering to pay, and Lydia observes the considerable amount of money the little boy had with him. As her fears return, she blames her for trusting the boy and worries that Beto is a cartel member. Deciding to confront him, she decides to interrogate on how come he was carrying so much money with him and from where the money was. Beto explains that he didn't steal that money, nor he got it from doing something illegal. He had received the payment as a reward for helping a man he had known from the dump, recover his gun and drugs.

Chapter 27 The Coyote

Using a payphone, the sisters call the coyote and request him to allow Lydia and Luca to cross the border together with them. He agrees after asking if the two extra people are in good shape and able to walk for a long distance. After deciding on a meeting point where he will come to meet them, the girls try to call their father and fail as they needed an international code that they didn't know.

Arriving at the meeting point, El Chacal is taken by surprise with the sister's beauty. Upon meeting the girls, he introduces himself to Lydia, Luca, and Beto, and at first, he refuses to take them with him because he never takes kids across the desert. In a short while, he changes his mind and agrees that they all join him in return for a massive amount of money—five thousand dollars for Lydia and Six thousand for each of the children.

Needing a bank to take out the money from her mother's deposit, Lydia is relieved to find a branch of her mother's bank nearby. After explaining the woman at the cashier desk why she needs to close her mother's account without having her death certificate, the cashier named Paola empathizes with Lydia and decides to help her while giving her an extra 500 pesos for Luca.

Chapter 28 Waiting to Cross The Desert

The apartment where El Chacal takes the group of migrants to wait till the time is right for them to cross the desert is nice and clean. In the kitchen, Lydia takes out all the money she had from the bank and hands it to the coyote. Because of the exchange rate being dismal, the money she has is not enough, and she is short of $372. Hearing about their problem from the other room, Beto offers to help them and gives El Chacal the rest of the money that Lydia and Luca needed.

The coyote informs them that as soon as the other group members arrive, they can begin the crossing.

Early the next morning, El Chacal brings in two young men and an older woman. Wishing to find out more about the newcomers, Lydia offers to prepare something to eat for everybody. The two men give her some money to buy the ingredients, and Lydia with Luca and the new woman head out to the shop. The woman introduces herself to Lydia.

Her name is Marisol, and she got deported to Mexico from California, where she was living with her two daughters. Having spent two months in detention, she was now determined to get back to her daughters. While heading back to the apartment, Lydia sees a sickle painted on the wall. Above it was an Owl. That was the sign of La Lechuza, and Lydia worries that Javier might find out where they are. Hurrying to get back in the house, Lydia is about to have another bad surprise as she finds Lorenzo there. Somehow he had managed to find them again, and he is planning to cross the desert with El Coyote also. Telling him that she saw signs of Los Jardineros around the city, Lydia sees how Lorenzo's posture changes, and his face gets paler, and she understands that he is afraid of the cartel too.

While women are cooking in the house, Soledad leaves the apartment and starts to pace the street outside, while wondering about the emptiness she sees on the other side of the border. Approaching the fence that separates her from El Norte, she sticks her hand in the dust on the other side, and while spitting through the fence, she felt that she had left a piece of herself on the American dirt.

Chapter 29 Choncho, Slim, David, Ricardin, and Nicholas

As they are all having dinner, Lorenzo seems preoccupied, and Lydia warns him that he should eat more if he wishes to survive the desert. When he asks her why she is so kind to him, she replies by telling him that she knows how bad it is to be afraid.

Later that night, Luca wakes up, frightened from a nightmare. Soon all the others will wake up also as they hear the sound of the keys in the lock. El Chacal arrives with five more people; two brothers named Choncho and Slim and their teenage sons David and Ricardin. A fifth is a man Nicholas who, like Marisol, got deported from the States where he was a Ph.D. student at the University of Arizona.

El Chacal tells them all to rest as much and also to prepare a suitcase with supplies, worm jackets for the night, and good shoes for walking. They are supposed to leave before sundown.

While waiting for the time to pass, the migrants fill the evening with cooking, cleaning around the house, and singing music. At the same time, Marison tells everybody the story of how she ended up deported from the United States. Knowing that it might take a long time till she will be able to check on her father again, Soledad calls the hospital to ask about his situation just to find out from Angela that he had died. Destroyed and unable to even cry, Soledad shakes in shock and tries to find a place to escape her panic. She knows that her sister won't be able to put up with this information as she had already been through too much and decides not to tell her anything until after they cross the desert.

Chapter 30 Preparing for Survival

The next day, El Chacal returns to the apartment and embarks them all in two pickup trucks. As Beto has nothing to pack, he is almost left behind by El Chacal, who has warned them all to bring warm coats for the cold desert nights. El Chacal prides himself on having all his migrants survive when crossing the desert with him, and he never agrees to take with him people that might not be able to get alive on the other side of the border. Beto's luck is that Nicolas has an extra jacket for the road, which he borrows to the little boy, so El Chacal allows him to continue his trip.

During the car ride, each of the migrants mentally prepares for the difficult days ahead of them. They were finding comfort in memories that bring them a little warmth and relief from all the struggles that they had been facing. Three hours after leaving the apartment, the pickup trucks stop in the middle of the desert, and from that point on, the migrants will need to start walking. El Coyote warns them about the rules they need to obey if they wish to survive the journey while also letting them know what to say in case they get caught. One after the other, aligned in the position that the coyote has assigned for each one of them, the migrants start walking in silence, under the clear night sky, and with only the light from the stars to guide them. These conditions are ideal for crossing the border the coyote tells them. After walking for one hour without talking anything, the group finds shelter under a rocky outcrop, and everybody tries to get some rest, but none of them manages to do so. They all pray in the dark, terrified by the strange sound and shadows they feel lurking around.

Are you enjoying the book so far?

If so, please help me reach more readers by taking 30 seconds to write just a few words on Amazon

Or, you can choose to leave one later...

Chapter 31 Border Patrol

Shortly after two o'clock in the morning, as they start walking again, El Chacal spots some pickup trucks that could belong either to a cartel or a "vigilante" group. They decide to hide for the rest of the night and wait for the vehicles to leave. As the trucks finally depart, the group can continue with their journey. The desert heat and the never-ending dunes get everyone exhausted, and the arrival at a water station was a welcoming feeling. Their moment of relaxation and chatter is suddenly interrupted as they all have to lie flat on the ground and hide from the sudden arrival of a Border patrol car. As the car passes them, they start moving again till they reach a safe spot, which is out of view and protected from the desert sun, where they can set the camp for the rest of the day.

Chapter 32 Left Behind

As soon as the sun sets, they get ready to depart again. El Chacal warns them about this part of the road being the most difficult as it will be eight miles of only rough terrain. He tells them that it will be a matter of life and death, and in case any of them will be unable to keep up with the group, they will be left behind. The alternative for the ones that cannot keep up with the group is to reach the Ruby Road, where they could eventually get found by the border patrol or the locals that are often passing by. The coyote starts moving at a brutal pace while their path winds around impassible sections that keep them away from the hiking trails and roads used by the border patrol. The beginning of the night finds them a few miles from Tumacacori-Carmen, where they set the camp in a cave-like formation. The migrants have no idea how close they are to Tucson, Arizona, from which they are only a forty-five-minute car ride.

As they are continuing their walk through an unknown canyon, a crack in the sky is followed by a sudden downpour, which gets them all soaked in no time. Luca feels an excruciating pain from a blister on one of his feet and finds it impossible to continue walking. Stopping to help Luca with the foot blister, Lydia and her son are left behind by the rest of the group. The night covering the desert is so dense and opaque that the two of them find themselves lost in a sea of darkness, unable to see and hear anything around. It is Luca's excellent orientation that saves them in the end, and the mother and child manage to find their group and get back in line with the others.

Chapter 33 Black Water

The downpour stops all of a sudden, the same way that it had started. All the migrants' clothes are completely wet, and the sharping cold of the desert night freezes them. Luca's teeth are shaking, and he feels so cold that he can almost hear his teeth shatter. El Chacal tells them that there is a blessing in the rain, and that comes from the fact that there will be fewer narcos and border patrols to venture on the roads when the weather is terrible.

All of a sudden, a sharp cry behind them makes them all duck in panic, and as turning towards the place the sound came from, they see a huge mass of black water approaching them from behind. Starting to run, they manage to escape the angry waters by climbing on a ledge. While helping the others climb, Ricardin is the last one to hop on, but the water catches him before having the chance to reach the safety of the higher ground. Barely managing to survive, one of his legs gets broken and stays behind the group. Choncho, his uncle, doesn't want to leave him alone in the desert and decides that they will try and reach the Ruby Road together.

Chapter 34 Protecting Each Other

Reaching a large cave where they can rest and dry their clothes, all the migrants think about the wounded man that they had to leave behind, and each one feels the guilt and regret. El Chacal tells them that they should all get undressed so that their clothes can dry faster and they do so by separating women inside and men outside the cave. While they are getting dry, Luca asks Lydia about the possibility that the two of them could stay together with Soledad, Rebeca, and even Beto once they arrive in the United States. Lydia considers the idea and imagines it as a real option, as she cannot imagine herself parting ways with the two sisters after all that they have been going through.

It is the migrants last night in the desert, and they can all hardly wait to arrive at the new lives that await them. As Rebeca leaves the cave in search of an isolated place to use as a toilet, Lorenzo follows her and tries to rape her.

Luckily El Chacal and Soledad find them just in time before anything could happen. Taking the gun from the hands of El Chacal, Soledad shoots and kills Lorenzo.

Chapter 35 Plot Uncovered

Fearing that somebody might have heard the gunshot, El Chacal returns to the cave and tells everybody to get ready to go. Before leaving, as a final act of kindness for Lorenzo, El Chacal decides to leave Lorenzo's wallet near him, in case somebody will find the dead body. While packing her stuff, Lydia finds Lorenzo's cell phone near the place where he was sleeping and decides to take it. As soon as she opens it, she sees that the many exchanges of messages he's been having with Javier since Lydia and Luca saw him the first time at the Migrant House in Huehuetoca. Realizing that Javier has been tracking their every move, Lydia decides to confront her family's assassin and calls him with the video from Lorenzo's phone. He is surprised to hear and see Lydia on the phone, and he tells her that his intention was never to see her dead. He just wanted her to suffer as much as he did when his daughter committed suicide. With all the force she had left, Lydia shouts to him and tells him that she doesn't plan to die, not as long as she has her son that she has to protect. She shows him after the body of Lorenzo and lets him know that it was her who killed him. Telling Javier *Goodbye,* she throws the phone in the sand while the camera still yawns at the vacant sky.

Chapter 36 Parting Ways

During the last part of the road, Beto finds it more and more difficult to control his asthma. Marisol understands what the little boy must be going through. Her daughter Daisy used to suffer from the same condition. In a final asthma attack, Beto dies while all the migrants gather around him in a last attempt to save his life. As they cannot carry his body through the remaining part of the road and offer him a proper burial, El Chacal promises to return and take care of the little boy's body. The remaining ten migrants and El Chacal manage to finally arrive at a remote campsite where two RVs are waiting for them. It is time that the coyote and migrants part ways from this point on, and they do so while also feeling that an essential part of them will always be left behind. It was this tumultuous time in the desert spent with strangers that created a sense of family.

Epilogue

Lydia sees Luca leaving for school each morning before starting the house cleaning job that she has been doing since she arrived in the States. They all live with the two sisters' cousin Cesar, his girlfriend, and her aunt, and everybody contributes to all the household chores. Whenever she has some free time, Lydia ventures to the local library in search of some books to read, this is her escape from the day to day life that unfolds monotonously. The sisters are also in the school but still struggling to get over the traumas that violently changed their lives forever.

Analysis of Key Characters

Lydia Quixano Perez – Lydia is a middle-class intellectual woman who has been living a charming and comfortable life in the sunny city of Acapulco. Owning a bookshop, she is passionate about reading. Being married to a kind and loving husband and having an eight-year-old son were some of Lydia's most significant accomplishments. The moment her life changes forever, her character will reveal some traits that she never knew she possessed. Understanding the great danger that she and her son where facing gives her the strength to suddenly leave everything behind and take immediate measures to save both of their lives. Throughout her journey, she will end up facing unexpected situations and people from different backgrounds, who will test her limits regarding her power to adjust and the ability to overcome the many obstacles that life threw towards her. At the same time, she will also find herself capable of showing compassion and kindness towards people that she had just met, proving that all the misfortune that had happened to her didn't have the power to turn her heart into stone.

Luca Quixano Perez – Luca is an eight-year-old boy who, despite his age, shows great maturity. Understanding his mother's struggles, he tries to be a support for her. No matter how hard their journey turns out to be, Luca never complains. Like his mother, he is also full of compassion for the two sisters that accompany them and shows a great solidarity spirit by not willing to leave them behind.

Rebeca and Soledad – Two teenage sisters, originating from Honduras who forcibly leave their family and entire life behind and escape to the United States. Both of them are very beautiful, especially Soledad, the older one, who's striking looks are attracting too much attention and put her life in danger. On top of her unique beauty, Soledad possesses an incredible strength of character. She is capable of sacrificing herself to protect the people that she loves the most. She is strong-willed, and her maturity overcomes her age. Her wish is to keep Rebeca safe from everything, and throughout their troubled journey, she will be both a maternal and paternal figure for her younger sister.

Major Symbols

The principal symbol that we encounter throughout the novel is the symbol of the owl. The owl or La Lechuza is the nickname given to Javier Crespo Fuentes head of the dominant cartel in Acapulco, Los Jardineros. Lechuza refers to a witch that turns into an owl in Mexican and Mexican-American folklore. The old woman shape-shifts into a giant owl, *La Lechuza*, to take revenge on people who wronged her during her life. Sometimes the owl is variously depicted as white and black, and sometimes it has the head of a woman.

Another symbol we may notice is the tattoos worn by all the members of the Los Jardineros cartel. These particular tattoos depict blood droplets, each droplet symbolizing a life taken.

Motifs

- The death train, La Bestia – the motif of survival
- Light and Dark - the battle of Good versus Evil
- Food – Nourishment and generosity
- Time – our relationship with the past and the future
- The rain in the desert – cleanse and rebirth

Themes

Many themes stand out in Cummin's book, but among them, there are a few which stand out:

- **The theme of family and family values** – Mexico is a country that places a lot of importance on strong family ties and traditions. The story looks at how different family members relate to each and the way they deal with the good and bad events that happen to them. Lydia's witnessing of her entire family getting killed breaks her entire core but at the same time pushes her to the limit in trying to save the only family member she has left, her son Luca

- **Love -** is one of the universal themes in literature, as in life. In *American Dirt*, Love proves to be both a force for good that inspires people to sacrifice themselves for others, but at the same time, a destructive and toxic force that drives people to madness or violence. Love is what pushes Lydia to fight so hard for Luca's life, but it's again Love, which causes Javier to search for revenge after his beloved daughter commits suicide because of Sebastian's article.

- **Revenge** – The need for revenge is as old as the world itself, and its many nuances are as diverse as the characters that it touches. What the author wishes to highlight in her novel is how revenge can ruin lives and cause destruction. Love disappears in the face of revenge, and so does everything else around. Revenge burns everything that it touches and never finds peace until there is nothing left behind.

- **Survival** – Cummin's book captivates the reader by its strong survival story, one in which the main characters must overcome countless odds to live another day.

Conclusion

A modern realism novel, *American Dirt*, was published in 2020 in the United States. The novel's story is exceptionally visual and dramatic. It has an incredible power to absorb the reader and make anyone that reads it to feel like they are part of the action. The narrative is very alert, and there is no breathing brake until reaching the end of the story. American Dirt is not a work of fiction but pure realism with just a change of names. The violence and cruelty depicted in the book are a daily reality in the lives of thousands of migrants that are leaving their homes in search of a better future. The characters are colorful, alive, and believable, and each one of them possesses individual and robust character features. Although the end brings the reader relief, the conclusion one may draw that *American Dirt* is far from having a happy ending. The main characters are safe for now but far from being fulfilled. Their futures will be hard, and their destiny uncertain.

Thought Provoking Discussion Questions About The Author Jeanine Cummins

- Who is Jeanine Cummins?
- What is the nationality of Cummins?
- Where was the author born?
- Where did Cummins spend her youth when growing up?
- When did she move back to the United States?
- When did Cummins marry her husband?
- How many books did Jeanine Cummins write?
- Why did Cummins have so much interest in the stories about immigration?

Discussion Questions About The Plot

- Why do Lydia and her son Luca need to escape from Mexico?
- What was the reason behind the murder of Lydia's family?
- What is the social climate in Acapulco at the time of the novel?
- How does Lydia plan to get out of Mexico?
- Where is Lydia planning to escape to?
- What is the nickname of the train that the migrants ride on their trip through Mexico?
- Where will the main protagonists live in the U.S.?

Discussion Questions About The Characters

- Who is Lydia Quixano Perez?

- Who is Javier Fuentes?

- Where are Rebeca and Soledad from?

- What was Sebastian's profession?

- What is the relationship between Lydia and Javier?

- Who are Lydia's and Luca's road companions?

- Who is the coyote that will help the group of migrants cross the desert?

Discussion Questions About Themes/Symbols/Motives

- Which are the main themes in *American Dirt?*
- How would you interpret the revenge theme of the book?
- What is the motif you find most striking?
- How would you describe the symbol of the owl?

THANK YOU FOR FINISHING THE BOOK!

Looks like you've enjoyed it! :)

We here at Cosmic Publications will always strive to deliver to you the highest quality guides. So, I'd like to thank you for supporting us and reading until the very end.

Before you go, would you mind leaving us a review on Amazon? It will mean a lot to us and support us creating high quality guides for you in the future. Just scan the QR code below.

Thank you again.
Warmly,

The Cosmic Publications Team